Shakespeare

WORK, LIFE AND TIMES

by Ann Donnelly and Elizabeth Woledge
The Shakespeare Birthplace Trust

Foreword

Welcome to the Shakespeare Birthplace Trust! Here, in and around Stratford-upon-Avon, we offer you entry into the historic and beautiful houses and gardens with which William Shakespeare was associated. He is the greatest of all writers, and the one who has the most universal appeal. Though he lived some four hundred years ago, his plays and poems still enthrall audiences worldwide. The power of his poetry and the depths of his understanding of the human condition transcend limitations of language and of space. Here at the Trust we aim to increase knowledge both of the material culture in which he lived and of the imaginative and intellectual heritage that he has left us.

Visitors to our houses and gardens, students of all ages attending our educational events, and scholars researching in our extensive collections and archives are welcomed and assisted by our expert and highly trained staff. We are proud of what we have to offer, and hope you will share our enthusiasm for Shakespeare and all he has given us.

Professor Stanley Wells, CBE, President

My love shall in my verse ever live young.

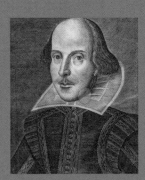

(*Sonnet 19*)

The Shakespeare Birthplace Trust

The Shakespeare Birthplace Trust was founded in 1847 by public subscription on a wave of public concern for the future of the Birthplace. In 1891 an Act of Parliament enshrined the Trust's purposes 'for the benefit of the nation' and today the Trust cares for five Tudor houses directly connected to Shakespeare and library, archive and museum collections of international importance.

At all of its properties and at The Shakespeare Centre, the Trust seeks to inspire and share a passion for Shakespeare through exhibitions, historic spaces and re-enactments, drama, poetry, classes, workshops and study days. The Trust also celebrates Shakespeare's national and international legacy by inviting collaboration with artists, writers, performers and centres for cultural expression around the world.

Leading the world's enjoyment of Shakespeare's works, life and times.

And yet to times in hope my verse shall stand,
Praising thy worth despite his cruel hand.

(*Sonnet 60*)

Support The Shakespeare Birthplace Trust

The Trust is an independent educational charity and receives no public subsidy or government funding. We depend entirely on income generated through our supporters: our visitors, volunteers, donors, Friends and all those who attend a course or shop in our retail outlets.

There are many ways to support and be part of the Trust's work:

- Volunteer with the Trust
- Join the Friends
- Visit the houses and Gift Aid your admission charge
- Make a purchase from the Trust's shops or online
- Attend events, lectures and courses
- Make a donation
- Leave a legacy to the Trust in your will.

Friends of the Trust enjoy:

- Free entry to Shakespeare's Houses and Gardens
- Exclusive Friends' events and outings
- 10% discount in our shops, mail order and online
- Discount on educational activities and events.

For more information go to www.shakespeare.org.uk or call +44 1789 204016.

Shopping

Each of our houses has a shop selling lots of truly unique, often locally sourced, gifts inspired by Shakespeare and his works.

- Every sale helps The Shakespeare Birthplace Trust achieve its objectives
- Each shop has its own individual theme and product range
- The Shakespeare Bookshop in Henley Street offers the widest possible range of Shakespeare books, DVDs and CDs
- Shop online for great gift ideas www.shakespeare.org.uk/onlineshop
- The gift of Friends membership available online.

Eating

In the cafes at Shakespeare's Birthplace, Hall's Croft, Anne Hathaway's Cottage and Mary Arden's Farm, visitors can enjoy a choice of traditional foods, many of which are sourced locally.

The Shakespeare Birthplace Trust is a registered educational charity. Charity Number 209302.

It's an honour and pleasure for me to serve as an Honorary Fellow of The Shakespeare Birthplace Trust, and to support its wonderful work in the presentation of the Shakespeare houses and in conservation and education. Joining the Friends is a practical and rewarding way to further the Trust's work and I urge all who love Shakespeare to do so.
Dame Judi Dench

By joining the Trust you can experience all that and more; and you can help to support the Trust's continuing work in interpreting the material life of Shakespeare's family in Stratford for future generations.
Michael Wood, Trustee

The story begins… Shakespeare's Stratford

I will tell you the beginning, and, if it please… you may see the end

(*As You Like It* Act 1, Scene 2)

Shakespeare's story begins in the heart of England, in Stratford-upon-Avon and the local Warwickshire villages of the Arden to the north and large open fields south of the River Avon, known as the Feldon.

A medieval grid pattern of streets is still preserved at the heart of the market town and despite four centuries of change, Shakespeare would have little trouble today in tracing the journey from his family home in Henley Street, past the homes of old friends, to his final resting place at Holy Trinity Church.

If he walked out of the family home [1] via the great front door next to the glover's workshop and left down Henley Street, he would soon pass the house (now the Birthplace gift shop) that belonged to neighbour and blacksmith Richard Hornby, whose children may have been his playmates as a young boy [2].

When he reached the top of Bridge Street, the scene would be less familiar but the street leads to the medieval stone Clopton Bridge [3], which still provides the southern entry to the town and the main crossing point of the River Avon. 28 Bridge Street was the house of his father's friend Henry Field, whose son Richard Field printed and published *Venus and Adonis* in London in 1593 [4].

On the corner of the High Street he would pass 'The Cage', the eventual home of his daughter Judith and her husband Thomas Quiney, a vintner and seller of tobacco (1 High Street) [5]. Cloth merchant Richard Quiney, Thomas' father and Shakespeare's friend, lived at 31 High Street [6]. Richard wrote the famous 'Quiney Letter' (right), so far the only surviving bit of Shakespearian correspondence. It is looked after in the archives of The Shakespeare Birthplace Trust. The front of 32 High Street is altered, but in Shakespeare's time it was home to Daniel Baker the linen-draper, a severe puritan who was responsible for banning players from the town when he was bailiff (mayor) in 1602 [7]. He was one of the narrow-minded and officious group of townsmen whom John Hall (Shakespeare's son-in-law) called 'foresworne villaines'. Further down the High Street, the ornately carved beams on the front of 'Harvard House', the home of butcher Thomas Rogers, would be very familiar to Shakespeare [8].

On Chapel Street, Shakespeare would pass the home of his friend July Shawe (now a shop) [9], who was witness to the signing of his will, and then Nash's House [10], the property of Thomas Nash, husband to Shakespeare's granddaughter Elizabeth, and the site of his grand house, New Place [11].

On crossing Walkers' Street (now Chapel Lane) he would walk by the Guild Chapel [12], where his father authorised the defacing of

To Shakespeare '*my loving countryman*'.

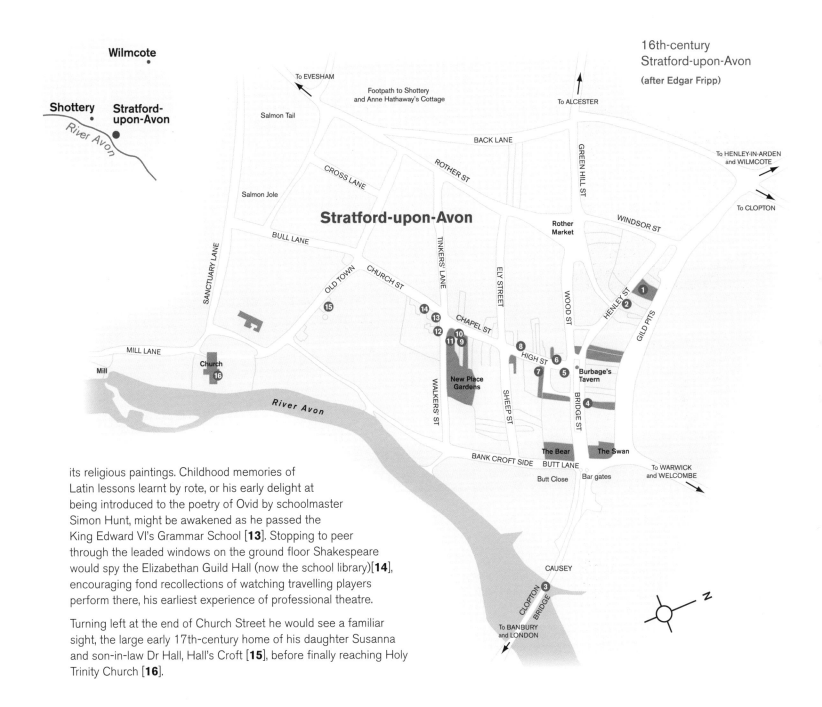

Wilmcote

To EVESHAM

Footpath to Shottery
and Anne Hathaway's Cottage

16th-century
Stratford-upon-Avon

(after Edgar Fripp)

To ALCESTER

Shottery   Stratford-
upon-Avon

River Avon

Salmon Tail

BACK LANE

To HENLEY-IN-ARDEN
and WILMCOTE

CROSS LANE

ROTHER ST

GREEN HILL ST

To CLOPTON

Salmon Jole

Stratford-upon-Avon

Rother
Market

WINDSOR ST

SANCTUARY LANE

BULL LANE

TINKERS' LANE

ELY STREET

WOOD ST

HENLEY ST

GILD PITS

OLD TOWN

CHURCH ST

15

14
13
12
11 10
9

CHAPEL ST

8

HIGH ST

6

1
2

MILL LANE

Church
16

WALKERS' ST

New Place
Gardens

SHEEP ST

7

5

Burbage's
Tavern

4

BRIDGE ST

Mill

River Avon

BANK CROFT SIDE   BUTT LANE

The Bear

The Swan

To WARWICK
and WELCOMBE

Butt Close   Bar gates

CAUSEY

CLOPTON BRIDGE
3

N

To BANBURY
and LONDON

its religious paintings. Childhood memories of
Latin lessons learnt by rote, or his early delight at
being introduced to the poetry of Ovid by schoolmaster
Simon Hunt, might be awakened as he passed the
King Edward VI's Grammar School [**13**]. Stopping to peer
through the leaded windows on the ground floor Shakespeare
would spy the Elizabethan Guild Hall (now the school library)[**14**],
encouraging fond recollections of watching travelling players
perform there, his earliest experience of professional theatre.

Turning left at the end of Church Street he would see a familiar
sight, the large early 17th-century home of his daughter Susanna
and son-in-law Dr Hall, Hall's Croft [**15**], before finally reaching Holy
Trinity Church [**16**].

Shakespeare's Birthplace

To you your father should be as a god,
One that composed your beauties, yea, and one
To whom you are but as a form in wax,
By him imprinted.

(*A Midsummer Night's Dream* Act 1, Scene 1)

SHAKESPEARE'S BIRTH

William Shakespeare was baptised at Holy Trinity Church, Stratford-upon-Avon, on 26 April 1564. The precise date of his birth is not known, but traditionally it is celebrated on 23 April, as it was customary to baptise an infant three days after birth.

Infant mortality in the 16th century was high and locally only one in three children survived into adulthood. Mary and John had already lost two baby girls. Bubonic plague struck Stratford shortly after William's birth, killing 15 per cent of the town's population. It is possible that Mary took her little boy to stay with her family in the comparative safety of rural Wilmcote, four miles away, until the threat of infection was over.

Death and An Infant, an engraving from *A Booke of Christian Prayers* by Richard Day.

The house today

Shakespeare's family home is a fascinating building. Documentary evidence allows us to trace in detail who owned the house and who lived there, from the time of William's parents, John and Mary Shakespeare, onwards.

Today the parlour, hall, workshop and bed chambers are furnished as they may have looked in 1574, when the house was full of children: William ten, Gilbert eight, Joan five, Anne three and baby Richard. Rare items of middle class 16th-century furniture are set in the context of carefully researched replica textiles and other domestic items, many of which are mentioned in Shakespeare's plays.

Petruccio

And here I'll fling the pillow, there the bolster, This way the coverlet, another way the sheets.

(*The Taming of the Shrew* Act 4, Scene 1)

The parish register entry of William's baptism.

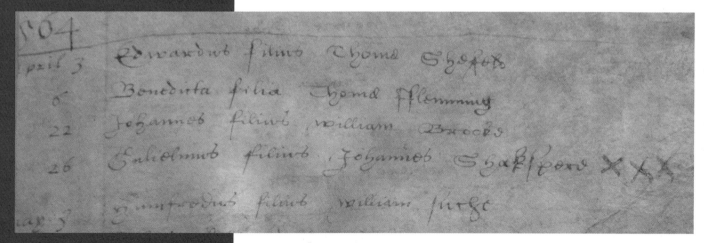

Facing page: Shakespeare's birthroom.

Young Shakespeare may have enjoyed some of the best professional theatrical performances of the day, in his home town.

Lord Leicester's Men visited the town in 1573–4 and 1576–7. The company was the most celebrated in the land. They commanded the premium performance fee of 15 shillings when they visited Stratford (most companies were only paid four or five shillings).

If he did manage to see a performance, William could not have failed to be impressed by the sumptuousness of the livery, costumes and props of these first-rate acting companies.

The family business

The Shakespeares' home doubled as a glover's shop for John at the eastern end of the building, with a barn and workshops in the backyard. Lime, alum, egg, dog excrement and urine were used to process the kid, lamb, dog and deer skins to make fine leather. John also sold his wares under the High Cross, one of two market crosses in the town.

About 20 years or so after the construction of the main house, a two-roomed cottage was added onto its western end. We know that Shakespeare's sister Joan and her husband William Hart, a hatter, lived there in the early 17th century, but it may have originally housed young Will, aged 18 and his new bride Anne, who was three months 'with child' with their daughter Susanna.

In 1601 William inherited the property from his father and it became an inn.

On his death in 1616 William Shakespeare left the property to his daughter Susanna Hall. His sister Joan Hart was allowed to live on in the small attached cottage for the rest of her life, for one shilling a year. After the death of his granddaughter, Elizabeth Barnard, the property passed to Joan's descendants and family ownership continued until the late 18th century.

Gloves were a major fashion accessory as worn by Shakespeare's patron, Henry Wriothesley, 3rd Earl of Southampton in the Tower of London (c. 1601–1603 from the original by John de Critz the Elder).

Shakespeare leased part of the property and it became a pub for many years.

A late 18th-century sketch of the Market Cross still at the corner of Bridge Street and High Street.

Facing page: tools in the glover's workshop.

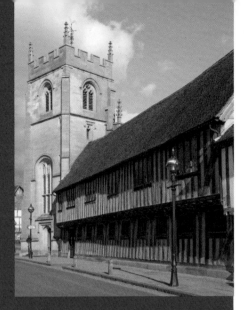

THE GRAMMAR SCHOOL AND GUILD HALL

Shakespeare's home was just a short walk from the town's grammar school, King's New School, on Church Street (now King Edward VI Grammar School) and the Guild Hall where his father attended meetings with other aldermen of the borough. The school was open to sons of members of the borough council, and it is likely that William enrolled there in 1571, when he was seven.

In *The Merry Wives of Windsor* he creates a comic scene with the schoolboy William reciting his Latin to his schoolmaster. Some of the Latin words sound like rude English ones and Mistress Quickly is shocked:

You do ill to teach the child such words […] and to call 'whorum'. Fie upon you!

(*The Merry Wives of Windsor* Act 4, Scene 1)

The Birthplace rescued

The house fell into decay during the first four decades of the 19th century and it was put up for sale. Following a national campaign in 1846, the Shakespeare Birthday Committee (later The Shakespeare Birthplace Trust), including such leading figures as Charles Dickens, finally raised the £3,000 necessary to buy the house for the nation in 1847. Dickens organised a series of amateur performances in London, Birmingham and Manchester, in which other noted contemporary literary figures featured, in an attempt to fund the purchase of the Birthplace.

The building was subsequently 'restored' in the 1860s to its appearance in a sketch of 1762 by Richard Greene. Many of the original internal structures, such as the hearths and rear window positions, remain intact.

Sale poster for Shakespeare's Birthplace, September 1847.

Richard Greene 1762 sketch of the Birthplace.

Birthplace garden

In the 16th century the area behind the Shakespeares' house would have served various practical purposes, partly in connection with John Shakespeare's glove-making and wool-dealing activities. Outbuildings for the storage of animal skins,

and liming pits were possibly sited there, together with a barn and a stable for a horse. The family is likely to have kept a pig and hens. They would also have grown a range of vegetables, herbs and fruit trees for cooking and medicine.

Today the garden layout dates from the mid-19th century and features many plants mentioned in Shakespeare's plays.

Shakespearian performances in the garden.

Shakespeare and the World

The languages you will hear during your visit to Shakespeare's Birthplace are a living testimony to his enduring international appeal.

In the garden you can see a bust of the great Indian poet and philosopher, Rabindranath Tagore, who was greatly inspired by Shakespeare's works. In The Shakespeare Centre there is a poem by the Muslim poet, Dr Sir Muhammad Iqbal, in English and Urdu:

**Though your own self remained hidden from the sight of all
Yet, your own eye could perceive the world unveiled.**

The Shakespeare Birthplace Trust Library contains translations of Shakespeare's work in over 70 languages.

Each year thousands of people take part in the traditional Shakespeare Birthday Celebrations in Stratford-upon-Avon and across the globe. Why not contact us and let us know how you mark Shakespeare's birthday, or find out how to get involved?

Go to www.shakespearesbirthday.org.uk

Tagore bust.

Mary Arden's Farm

WILMCOTE

They say he is already in the Forest of Ardenne,
and a many merry men with him; and there
they live like the old Robin Hood of England.
They say many young gentlemen flock to him
every day, and fleet the time carelessly,
as they did in the golden world.

(*As You Like It* Act 1, Scene 1)

A CASE OF MISTAKEN IDENTITY

From the late 18th century until recent times Shakespeare's mother's home, 'Mary Arden's House', was believed to be the 16th-century half-timbered building we now refer to as 'Palmer's Farm'.

When The Shakespeare Birthplace Trust commissioned in-depth research into the history of the house in 2000 an exciting discovery came to light: the Arden farm was in fact the farm next door!

Fortunately, Mary Arden's true home had been rescued from likely demolition by the Trust in the 1960s, and the farm was already open to the public under its 19th-century name, 'Glebe Farm'.

The farm that Shakespeare knew

Shakespeare would have spent time as a boy in Wilmcote, playing and helping out with tasks around the farm where his step-grandmother, Agnes Arden, lived. In the long evenings, sitting with the old lady by the light of the fire, he no doubt heard her tell traditional tales of Robin Hood, George and the Dragon, The Dun Cow, and Robin Goodfellow.

Wilmcote is situated to the north-west of the River Avon, an area traditionally known as 'The Forest of Arden'. By Shakespeare's time the forest had long gone. Shakespeare's maternal grandfather, Robert Arden, was a wealthy farmer and held about 70 acres of land in Wilmcote and some more in Snitterfield, which he rented to Richard Shakespeare, Shakespeare's paternal grandfather.

Mary Arden's personal seal on a land settlement depicts a rearing horse, indicating that her father may have bred horses.

The farmstead we see today is essentially a Victorian/Edwardian one, but embedded into the fabric of the house is evidence of Robert's original early 16th-century home.

Mary Arden was clearly bright. When she was about 17 (the youngest of eight sisters), her father chose her to be an executor of his will, in which he left her property in Wilmcote and other land holdings. She married John Shakespeare in around 1557.

A reconstruction drawing illustrating the likely appearance of Mary Arden's house in Robert Arden's time.

Repairing boots.

Facing page: traditional wool spinning.

Palmer's Farm

Adam Palmer was a close friend of William's parents and grandparents.

This building today retains much of its original 16th-century structure. Visitors can witness traditional farming methods, meet the animals, learn about age-old customs and even try their hand at domestic skills.

In Shakespeare's time Adam Palmer would have employed several day-labourers to undertake the daily work on the land and the care of livestock, and female servants to help his wife with domestic and farmyard tasks.

In *As You Like It*, the court jester, Touchstone, reflects with comic sentiment on a love affair he once had with a country maid: **'I remember the kissing of her batlet and the cow's dugs that her pretty chapped hands had milked'** (Act 2, Scene 4). The cow's 'dugs' are its udders and the maid's 'batlet' was the wooden club she used for beating the washing.

Domestic chores.

Given Palmer's wealth, the house was relatively modest in size, with four bedchambers, two parlours, a hall and a kitchen. The decorative closed studded timbering on the outside of the building would have signalled to the community that he enjoyed a degree of affluence. His few luxury items included feather beds, pewter and brass worth over £3 (used to cover tables and chests), one and a half dozen cushions and silver valued at £6.

An early 17th-century 'truckle bed' for children or servants that wheeled under the main bed when not in use.

By 1584 Palmer had improved his house, demolishing the old hall and parlour to the eastern end and building a new hall, cross-passage and kitchen, to create the building that can be seen today.

An English 16th-century oak cupboard with carved doors.

Facing page: Palmer's Farm.

Farmland and gardens

Functional but attractive rural gardens provided the farmers' wives with a 'medical chest' for the treatment of household ailments, a convenient supply of vegetables for cooking, and sweet-smelling flowers and herbs to decorate the home.

The local farmland in the 16th century would have been a mixture of cultivated arable and grazing pasture surrounded by woods and common land popular for hunting.

Today Mary Arden's Farm revives all the sights, smells and sounds of these times with traditional land stewardship including ridge and furrow ploughing with working horses, hedge-laying and orchards conserving old fruit varieties. Rare breed animals roam the grounds freely and visitors can explore the nature trails and admire the abundant wildlife – woodpeckers, rabbits, deer and more – all attracted by specially created habitats to preserve indigenous species.

I Have Choice For My Kitchen, a painting depicting early 17th-century foodstuffs.

Mealtime, Tudor style.

A real working Tudor farm.

Hunting tapestry from a bed valance made locally in Shakespeare's period.

Shakespeare and Hunting

This was a popular country pursuit in Shakespeare's time, especially for the well-to-do. He refers to hunting and falconry many times, most disturbingly in *The Taming of the Shrew*.

In Act 4, Scene 1, Petruccio refers to his future wife Kate as being like a wild bird:

Petruccio
Thus have I politicly begun my reign,
And 'tis my hope to end successfully.
My falcon now is sharp and passing empty,
And till she stoop she must not be full-gorged,
For then she never looks upon her lure.

Birds of prey need always to be kept hungry otherwise they fly away, so Petruccio decides to starve Kate…

Petruccio and Kate, *The Taming of the Shrew*, RSC 1978.

Anne Hathaway's Cottage

SHOTTERY

And yet, by heaven, I think my love as rare
As any she belied with false compare.

(Sonnet 130)

HAND-FASTING

It is possible that William and Anne 'plighted their troth' in a hand-fasting ceremony. This was traditionally undertaken on Lammas Day (1 August) where an exchange of vows was witnessed and the couple bedded, prior to the official church wedding.

Measure for Measure is partly about a hand-fasting. Claudio has been hand-fasted to his lover Julietta and between this ceremony and the church wedding she becomes pregnant. For this 'crime' of fornication he is imprisoned and sentenced to death. His justification (below) is that his hand-fasting made him and Julietta man and wife in the eyes of God and thus no sin was committed.

**Upon a true contract
I got possession of Julietta's bed.
You know the lady; she is fast my wife.**

(*Measure for Measure* Act 1, Scene 2)

Shakespeare is dramatising a debate as to whether hand-fasting was as legally and morally binding as a formal wedding.

Rural Shottery

Alongside the peaceful banks of Shottery brook stands Anne Hathaway's Cottage. The small wooded valley is now an oasis of calm on the outskirts of Stratford. In Shakespeare's day this now built-up area consisted of fields and farms.

It was an exceptional harvest in late August 1582. The farming community of Shottery would have toiled in the open fields. When the last sheaf had been gathered in, it would have been cause for a celebration, the 'harvest home'. William, an 18 year-old youth with a lust for life's experiences, possibly joined in with the feasting and drinking, as the Hathaways were close family friends of the Shakespeares.

Anne Hathaway

Anne was the daughter of Richard Hathaway, a well-to-do yeoman farmer. When he died in 1581, he left his 25 year-old daughter a dowry of £6 13s 4d, a considerable sum.

The charms of the charismatic youth from Stratford, with his quick and easy wit, would have been attractive to any woman. Nine months after the harvest, Anne Hathaway gave birth to their first daughter, Susanna, following a rushed marriage in November. Shakespeare was one of only three men who married before they were 20 and the only one of these whose bride was pregnant.

**Be not afraid, good youth, I will not have you;
And yet when wit and youth is come to harvest
Your wife is like to reap a proper man.**

(*Twelfth Night, or What You Will* Act 3, Scene 1)

Harvest scene from a book known to Shakespeare; Raphael Holinshead, *The Chronicles of England, Scotland and Ireland, 1577.*

Facing page: original passage from the hall.

SHAKESPEARE'S 'COURTING CHAIR'?

In the second bedchamber there is a remarkable armchair. The chair was first recorded as being in the house in 1792 by travel writer, Samuel Ireland, who illustrated it for the first travel guide of Warwickshire. Ireland bought it from the Hathaways and took it back to London. In 2002 it resurfaced in an auction house, was bought by The Shakespeare Birthplace Trust and was returned to the cottage.

Mr Hart of Stratford (a descendant of Shakespeare's sister Joan) told Ireland that the chair had always been known as 'Shakespeare's Courting Chair' and that it had been passed down from Shakespeare to his granddaughter, Lady Elizabeth Barnard, and from her to the Hathaway family.

The chair back is carved with two elements from the Shakespeare coat of arms; a shield with a spear and a falcon holding a spear. Analysis of the layers of wax/dirt on the chair suggests that these carvings were added shortly after the chair was made in the early 17th century. The initials 'W.A.S.' were added some time after Ireland bought the chair, and may have been carved by his son, William Henry, an infamous forger of 'Shakespeare documents'.

A hurried wedding

Anne and William's wedding arrangements were fraught with problems. William had to ask his father's consent to marry as he was still a minor. To avoid scandal it was important that the marriage took place before signs of Anne's pregnancy became too obvious. To speed proceedings William had to apply to the Bishop's Court in Worcester. Two Shottery farmers, Fulke Sandells and John Richardson, accompanied William to the court and gave surety of the huge sum of £40 for the bond, to be paid if the marriage proved invalid.

The clerk responsible made the careless mistake of writing 'Anne Whateley of Temple Grafton' instead of 'Anne Hathaway of Shottery', but her name was entered correctly on the licence bond.

William was 18 when he married and Anne 26; as such their match was unusual. In *Twelfth Night* the Duke Orsino gives two pieces of advice about respective ages of marriage partners.

Firstly:

**Let still the woman take
An elder than herself. So wears she to him;
So sways she level in her husband's heart.**

Or, alternatively:

**Then let thy love be younger than thyself,
    Or thy affection cannot hold the bent.**

> (*Twelfth Night, or What You Will* Act 2, Scene 4)

Orsino thinks that men should marry women younger than themselves; the traditional pattern.

It is not known what William did to support his wife and child. Two years later Shakespeare and Anne became parents again, this time of twins, Hamnet and Judith, named after the couple's friends, baker Hamnet Sadler and his wife Judith, who lived on the corner of High Street and Sheep Street. The couple in turn named their own son William. Sadly the male twin, Hamnet, died when he was only eleven leaving Judith to survive alone into adulthood and old age (she died aged 77).

A 16th-century wedding.

WEDDING CUSTOMS

On her wedding day Anne would have worn her best set of clothes, with her hair worn loose and crowned with a garland of herbs such as rosemary. She would have been escorted by her bridesmaids who would spread rushes before her to protect her shoes and clothes from the mud of the rutted road to church. William would have dressed in his finest doublet and hose, and been escorted by his male friends to the bride's house with the musical accompaniment of the pipe and tabor. The groom usually bought gloves for wedding guests (an appropriate gift as Shakespeare's father's was a glover) in exchange for herbs and flowers.

The ceremony began at the door of the church and the ring was blessed. Afterwards the wedding party entered the main body of the church for the nuptial mass.

Wife and muse?

One of Shakespeare's earliest sonnets might have been written for Anne, possibly his earliest surviving poem. There is a pun on Anne's name in the final two lines.

Sonnet 145

Those lips that love's own hand did make
Breathed forth the sound that said 'I hate'
To me that languished for her sake;
But when she saw my woeful state,
Straight in her heart did mercy come,
Chiding that tongue that ever sweet
Was used in giving gentle doom,
And taught it thus anew to greet:
'I hate' she altered with an end,
That followed it as gentle day
Doth follow night who, like a fiend,
From heaven to hell is flown away.
    'I hate' from hate away she threw,
    And saved my life, saying, 'not you.'

'Hate away' was a pronunciation of 'Hathaway'; 'And' sounds like 'Anne'.

'The Hathaway Bed', a late 16th-century tester bed (a bed with a canopy) given to the Hathaway family by Shakespeare's granddaughter, Elizabeth Barnard. Richard Hathaway's will of 1581 specified that this and another bed were to remain in the house during the lifetime of his wife Joan, son Bartholomew and son John.

The structure of the original 1460s house can clearly be seen on the first floor: a 'cruck' frame, consisting of a pair of massive curved oak timbers supporting the roof and walls, which are made of wattle and daub (woven hazel covered in a mixture of mud, dung and chopped straw).

The house

Anne Hathaway's Cottage was actually a farmhouse. In Anne's girlhood it consisted of the lower half of the current building, next to the road. Visitors still enter the house through the original front doorway and into the cross-passage. To the right of the passage was a kitchen, and to the left, a hall that was open to the roof (the chimneys were inserted later).

Early in the 17th century when the premises were owned by Bartholomew Hathaway, Anne's brother, a taller section was added to the house at the orchard end.

The house remained in the Hathaway family for several generations, through the descendants of Anne's brother. The male line became extinct in 1746 on the death of John Hathaway.

Mary Baker, a distant descendant, was still living there in 1892, when The Shakespeare Birthplace Trust purchased the property. With it came various items of family furniture, including the Hathaway Bed, dating from Anne's time. Mary Baker became the first custodian of the house. The cottage has changed little since she died in 1899.

Mary Baker's bonnet, the chair she sat on and the table in the photograph (below left) are still in Anne Hathaway's Cottage, along with Anne Hathaway's family furniture.

Mary Baker, the first custodian of the cottage.

The hall/parlour.

Anne Hathaway's Cottage gardens

In Anne's girlhood, the 'cottage' garden would have been more of a farmyard than a flower garden. The quintessential 'English cottage garden' dates from the late 19th century, but during Anne and William's courtship the surrounding meadows and the banks of the brook would have had wild flowers in abundance.

**Eternity was in our lips and eyes,
Bliss in our brow's bent**

(*Antony and Cleopatra*
Act 1, Scene 3)

Today this award-winning landscape delights visitors from around the world with its traditional plants and flowers and the popular Shakespeare-themed sculpture and tree gardens.

Sculpture garden.

Shakespeare and Love

Shakespeare's sonnets combine intense thought with deep emotions.

Shall I compare thee to a summer's day?
Thou art more lovely and more temperate.
Rough winds do shake the darling buds of May,
And summer's lease hath all too short a date.
Sometime too hot the eye of heaven shines,
And often is his gold complexion dimmed.
And every fair from fair sometime declines,
By chance or nature's changing course untrimm'd;
But thy eternal summer shall not fade
Nor lose possession of that fair thou ow'st,
Nor shall death brag thou wander'st in his shade
When in eternal lines to time thou grow'st.
    So long as men can breathe or eyes can see,
    So long lives this, and this gives life to thee.

(*Sonnet 18*)

This is perhaps the most famous sonnet of them all. The word 'sonnet' comes from the Italian 'sonnetto' meaning 'little sounds.'

Try whispering this one slowly into the ear of someone you love; or try imagining it as being addressed to yourself and read aloud very softly!

Love's Labour's Lost,
RSC 2008.

New Place, Nash's House and Harvard House

Lowliness is young ambition's ladder,
Whereto the climber-upward turns his face.

(*Julius Caesar* Act 2, Scene 1)

NASH'S
HOUSE
AND
THE SITE OF
NEW PLACE

Fame and fortune

During the late 1580s/early 1590s, Shakespeare left Stratford to seek his fortune in London, leaving his wife and young children in Henley Street.

In 1593 Shakespeare obtained the patronage of a glamorous young patron, Henry Wriothesley, the 3rd Earl of Southampton, to whom he dedicated his first published poem *Venus and Adonis* and *The Rape of Lucrece* the following year. The poems proved to be a great hit among readers and were the most successful of Shakespeare's publications. Many editions were issued during his lifetime. The printer was fellow Stratfordian, Richard Field (probably an old school friend), who had also moved to London and was based in Blackfriars.

By 1592, Shakespeare had become an established player and playwright in London and author of at least seven plays. In 1594 he helped to found the Lord Chamberlain's Men and held shares in the company.

Five years later he had amassed sufficient wealth to afford a new family home back in Stratford, the second largest house in town, known as 'New Place', bought from William Underhill for about £120.

Buying New Place

In 1597 'New Place', or 'the Great House' as it was also known, became Shakespeare's grand home. It was a medieval house built around 1490 by Hugh Clopton in Chapel Street (opposite the Guild Chapel) and described by John Leland (librarian to Henry VIII) as being 'a pretty house of brick and timber'.

By 1598, Shakespeare had been ranked as one of the most prosperous men in Stratford. From the list of chief householders in Chapel Ward, where New Place was situated, we find that out of 20 holders of corn, only two have more in stock than William Shakespeare.

The best-loved books fall to pieces.
One copy of the first edition survives intact;
here is one surviving page from another.

THE SHAKESPEARE COAT OF ARMS

In 1596 Shakespeare arranged the grant of a coat of arms on behalf of his father from the College of Heralds. This grant was based on the service of John's ancestors and his association with the Arden family, and entitled him (and his heir William) to the status of 'gentleman'.

The coat of arms is included on Shakespeare's monument in Holy Trinity church, erected by 1623.

Non Sanz Droict (Not Without Right)

The same year, Richard Quiney wrote a letter addressed to Shakespeare appealing to him, possibly on the borough's behalf, for financial help. Later, Alderman Sturley wrote to Quiney suggesting that he should encourage Shakespeare to complete a purchase of land at Shottery, to secure certain private and public benefits.

Shakespeare made several investments in Stratford, including in 1602 an estate of 107 acres of land in the open fields of Old Stratford, for which he paid £320, a considerable sum of money in the Elizabethan era.

We do not know how much time Shakespeare spent with his family at home in Stratford, but it is likely that he moved back there frequently, especially when London's theatres were closed.

New Place 'fine' for £60 establishing legal entitlement to purchase property.

The house

A 17th-century sketch of the New Place site shows a gabled, half-timbered gatehouse that opened onto Chapel Street, in front of a grassy courtyard and the main medieval brick house. The neighbourhood was a pleasant and peaceful one. To the rear of the house were barns and elm trees, and on the other side of the lane was the Guild Garden with its orchard, bowling green, dovecote, herb garden and fountain.

It is thought that the servants lived in the attic floor with gabled windows and that the first floor was used as a long gallery. New Place was very spacious and could easily accommodate extra guests. It is likely that Shakespeare penned many of his plays in his study here from 1597.

Following Shakespeare's death in April 1616, New Place and Shakespeare's other properties passed to ownership of his eldest daughter Susanna and her husband Dr John Hall. The couple moved into the family home, but it is likely that Anne continued to live on in part of the house.

An artist/historian's impression of New Place by Pat Hughes, 1995.

DEATH OF SHAKESPEARE'S SON

A year before moving to New Place, Shakespeare and Anne had suffered the devastating blow of the death of their son Hamnet, Judith's twin brother, aged eleven. The register entry records Hamnet Shakespeare's burial in Stratford on 11 August 1596. Shakespeare is thought to have been writing, or reworking, *King John* at that time, where he writes movingly about a mother's grief for her young son.

**Grief fills the room up of my absent child,
Lies in his bed, walks up and down with me,
Puts on his pretty looks, repeats his words,
Remembers me of all his gracious parts,
Stuffs out his vacant garments with his form.**
(*King John* Act 3, Scene 4)

Elizabeth Hall and Nash's House

Elizabeth Hall (later Nash) was the only grandchild Shakespeare would ever know. She was eight years old when he died. She went on to marry Thomas Nash, who owned the house that directly adjoined her grandfather's New Place. She was married to Nash for 20 years before he died. Her second marriage was to John (later Sir John) Barnard. The couple inherited New Place from her parents, but they chose to live at Abington Manor in Northamptonshire. When Elizabeth died childless in 1670, Shakespeare's direct line of descent ended.

When the Clopton family again became owners of New Place, in the second half of the 17th century, they substantially rebuilt the front of the property. The house was finally demolished in 1759 by the Reverend Francis Gastrell.

In 1876, The Shakespeare Birthplace Trust assumed responsibility for Nash's House and the site of New Place.

New Place gardens

When Shakespeare bought New Place it stood in extensive grounds. His property deeds mention two gardens and two orchards. This estate continues to be used as a garden and now features an Elizabethan-style knot garden, with trellis-work which was created in 1919–20. The four beds or 'knots' incorporate an interweaving design of herbs and shrubs, based on illustrations in the gardening books of Shakespeare's time. Beyond, in the 'Great Garden', is an aged mulberry tree (said to have been grown from a cutting taken from a tree planted by Shakespeare). Today it contains a range of Shakespeare-inspired sculptures by Greg Wyatt, supported by the Newington-Cropsey Foundation.

Shakespeare's New Place

The site of New Place, its gardens and Nash's House are closed for the creation of a major new heritage landmark which will be at the centre of the worldwide celebrations of 400 years of Shakespeare's legacy in 2016.

Shakespeare's New Place was the only family home that Shakespeare ever purchased. Due to re-open in April 2016 it will be the contemporary jewel in the crown of our national literary and cultural heritage. Visitors will walk in Shakespeare's footsteps and discover the story of the family man and businessman at the height of his fame in his home town of Stratford-upon-Avon.

The New Place project is supported by the Heritage Lottery Fund and English Heritage.

Harvard House

Harvard House was built by local businessman Thomas Rogers in 1596; his initials and those of his second wife, Alice, are carved into the front of the building. The following year William Shakespeare purchased New Place, the largest house in the centre of Stratford-upon-Avon.

The two families would certainly have known each other. Thomas Rogers was a successful butcher and a corn and cattle merchant. He served as Bailiff and Alderman for the Stratford Corporation, as did John Shakespeare, William's father. The elaborately carved front of the building is a statement of Rogers' wealth and social standing within the local community.

The house remained in the Rogers family until about 1670. After being sold, it was occupied by a variety of tradesman until the early 1900s. Following restoration, the house was presented in 1909 to Harvard University.

THE AMERICAN CONNECTION

Thomas Rogers' daughter, Katherine, married Robert Harvard of Southwark, London, in Holy Trinity Church, Stratford-upon-Avon in 1605.

The couple lived in London, where their children were born. Plague hit the city in 1625 and in the Harvard household only Katherine and two of her sons, John and Thomas, survived.

Now a property owner, Katherine was able to send John to Cambridge University. John Harvard married Ann Sadler and in 1637 they settled in Massachusetts, USA. John worked as a minister and teacher, and died of tuberculosis on 14 September 1638.

Before his death, the Massachusetts Bay Colony established a fund for the founding of a college. John had inherited a large amount of money from his family and left £750 – in excess of £3 million today – and his library of 230 books. The college was named after him and still remains part of Harvard University today.

The Shakespeare Birthplace Trust has cared for Harvard House on behalf of Harvard University since 1990.

Hall's Croft

If thou couldst, doctor, cast
The water of my land, find her disease,
And purge it to a sound and pristine health.

(*Macbeth* Act 5, Scene 3)

A doctor 'casting the waters'
(examining a patient's urine sample).

John Hall

John Hall proved a wealthy and dependable son-in-law, only eleven years Shakespeare's junior. He was a physician of some renown and his case notes were published after his death in 1657, a popular textbook for other doctors for many years. The casebook provides a valuable insight into the medical practice of the period.

Hall came from a medical family in Bedfordshire. He was a churchwarden and Holy Trinity Church played a very important part in his life. Puritan by persuasion, Hall kept a keen eye on the behaviour of fellow parishioners, making reports on such 'beastly behaviour' as a man 'sleeping in the belfry, with his hat on, upon the Sabbath'.

Dost thou think, because thou art virtuous, there shall be no more cakes and ale?

(*Twelfth Night, or What You Will* Act 2, Scene 1)

Dr Hall was a compassionate and diligent physician, treating both rich and poor, Catholic and Protestant, alike.

Some physicians practised astronomy, others blood-letting. John Hall's preference was for treatments made from plants, herbs, animal extracts, gemstones and rocks. The garden at the back of Hall's Croft is planted with many of the herbs mentioned in Hall's medical notebook.

I ever
Have studied physic, through which secret art,
By turning o'er authorities, I have,
Together with my practice, made familiar
To me and to my aid the blest infusions
That dwells in vegetives, in metals, stones.

(*Pericles* Act 3, Scene 12)

The main part of this fine timbered building was put up in 1613. For most of its history, it has been the home of prosperous, often professional people and in the mid-19th century served as a small school. The Trust purchased the building in 1949 and, after substantial repairs and alterations, opened it to the public in 1951.

The title page of John Gerard's *Herbal*, 1597.

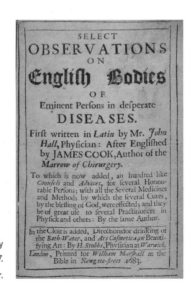

Select Observations on English Bodies by John Hall, published by James Cooke, 1657.
Facing page: the parlour.

THE 'WS' RING

Nearly two hundred years after William Shakespeare's death, an Elizabethan seal ring, made of gold and bearing the initials 'WS', was discovered by labourers in a field just outside the grounds of Holy Trinity Church, Stratford-upon-Avon.

Could this have been Shakespeare's lost signet ring? Shakespeare's last will and testament was amended on 25 March 1616 indicating that he had lost his seal ring:

'In Witness whereof I have hereunto put my ~~Seale~~ hand ..'

An Elizabethan man's gold signet ring, with the initials 'WS' entwined with a 'true-lover's' knot.

Medicine and Shakespeare's plays

Shakespeare's representation of doctors varies tremendously. There are comic doctors, like Dr Caius in *The Merry Wives of Windsor*, written in 1597, whose French accent renders his attempts to join in with town life absurd. For instance when he wishes to join two friends he says **'I shall make-a the turd'** (Act 3, Scene 3). But there are also gifted doctors like Cerimon in *Pericles*, which was written in 1607, the year of Dr Hall's

John Hall's dispensary.

marriage to Susanna. Cerimon finds more pleasure in his ability to **'speak of the disturbances / That nature works, and of her cures'** than in **'tott'ring honour'** (Act 3, Scene 3). It is Cerimon who miraculously restores the apparently dead queen to life and hence provides the play with its happy ending.

Susanna Hall

Shakespeare's eldest child was clearly strong in character. Her public reputation, and no doubt her relationship with John Hall, were to be severely tested when she was accused by a young man named John Lane of having an affair with the hatter, Rafe Smith, and of his contracting 'the runinge of the rayne' (a venereal infection). Susanna brought an action against Lane for slander in the church court, but he failed to turn up for the hearing and the case was closed.

Part of her epitaph (possibly by her daughter Elizabeth) reads:

**Witty above her sex, but that's not all
 Wise to salvation was good Mistress Hall.
    Something of Shakespeare was in that, but this
    Wholly of him with whom she's now in bliss.**

Holy Trinity Church

Holy Trinity Church in Stratford-upon-Avon marks most of the major landmarks of Shakespeare's life, from the cradle to the grave.

His gravestone is located in the chancel together with those of his wife Anne, daughter Susanna and her husband John Hall, and his granddaughter's first husband, Thomas Nash.

Shakespeare's grave is engraved with a blessing and a curse:

**Good friend, for Jesus' sake forbear
To dig the dust enclosed here:
Blessed be the man that spares these stones,
And cursed be he that moves my bones.**

A memorial bust compares Shakespeare to Nestor, Socrates and Virgil for his eloquence, oratory and poetry.

We do not know the cause of Shakespeare's death but there was an outbreak of fever (most likely typhus) in the year he died, as recorded by John Hall.

Hall's Croft gardens

A range of fresh medicinal plants would have been required for John Hall's elaborate herbal preparations, and it is very likely that he would have cultivated these close to the house. A formal bed established in 1999 contains many of these herbs. The modern walled garden was created in the early 20th century and boasts fragrant and mature herbaceous borders and an old mulberry tree.

Memorial bust at Holy Trinity Church.

Shakespeare and Family Life

Hall's Croft is a reminder to us that Shakespeare's plays are full of family intrigues and tensions. Some things never change! Just as Susanna Hall's reputation was tested, so too are those of the merry wives of Windsor; Mistress Ford and Mistress Page. One of Shakespeare's most popular characters, the fat knight Sir John Falstaff, tries to woo them both at once but is himself tricked and disappointed. At one point the two wives help him to escape the wrath of the jealous Master Ford in a laundry basket which is dropped into the Thames. Later, Falstaff comically reflects:

Well, if I be served such another trick, I'll have my brains ta'en out and buttered, and give them to a dog for a New Year's gift. [...] You may know by my size that I have some alacrity in sinking.

(*The Merry Wives of Windsor* Act 3, Scene 5)

Shakespeare is definitely not politically correct when it comes to making fun of Falstaff's size, and he does so time and again – and therein lies the humour!

Falstaff, *Merry Wives of Windsor*, RSC 1996.

Shakespeare's history

The Shakespeare Family Tree

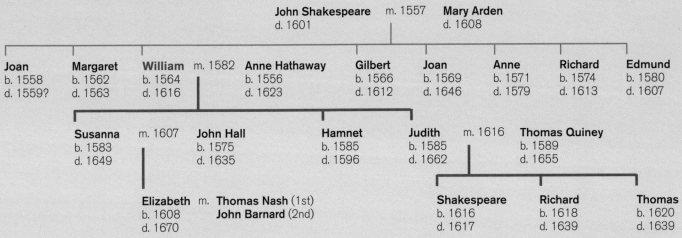

John Shakespeare m. 1557 **Mary Arden**
d. 1601   d. 1608

Joan | **Margaret** | **William** m. 1582 **Anne Hathaway** | **Gilbert** | **Joan** | **Anne** | **Richard** | **Edmund**
b. 1558 | b. 1562 | b. 1564 | b. 1556 | b. 1566 | b. 1569 | b. 1571 | b. 1574 | b. 1580
d. 1559? | d. 1563 | d. 1616 | d. 1623 | d. 1612 | d. 1646 | d. 1579 | d. 1613 | d. 1607

Susanna m. 1607 **John Hall** | **Hamnet** | **Judith** m. 1616 **Thomas Quiney**
b. 1583 | b. 1575 | b. 1585 | b. 1585 | b. 1589
d. 1649 | d. 1635 | d. 1596 | d. 1662 | d. 1655

Elizabeth m. **Thomas Nash** (1st)
b. 1608 | **John Barnard** (2nd)
d. 1670

Shakespeare | **Richard** | **Thomas**
b. 1616 | b. 1618 | b. 1620
d. 1617 | d. 1639 | d. 1639

Shakespeare and his times

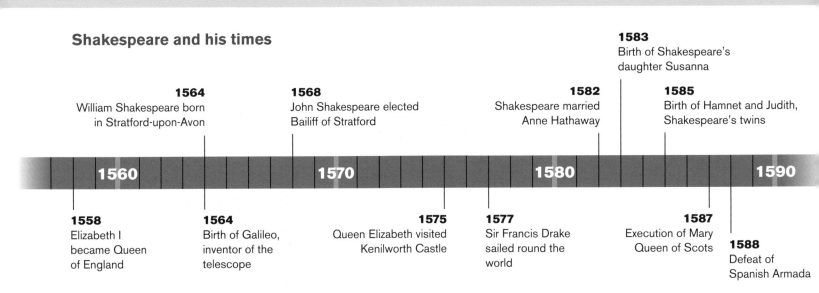

1583
Birth of Shakespeare's
daughter Susanna

1564
William Shakespeare born
in Stratford-upon-Avon

1568
John Shakespeare elected
Bailiff of Stratford

1582
Shakespeare married
Anne Hathaway

1585
Birth of Hamnet and Judith,
Shakespeare's twins

1560 | **1570** | **1580** | **1590**

1558
Elizabeth I
became Queen
of England

1564
Birth of Galileo,
inventor of the
telescope

1575
Queen Elizabeth visited
Kenilworth Castle

1577
Sir Francis Drake
sailed round the
world

1587
Execution of Mary
Queen of Scots

1588
Defeat of
Spanish Armada

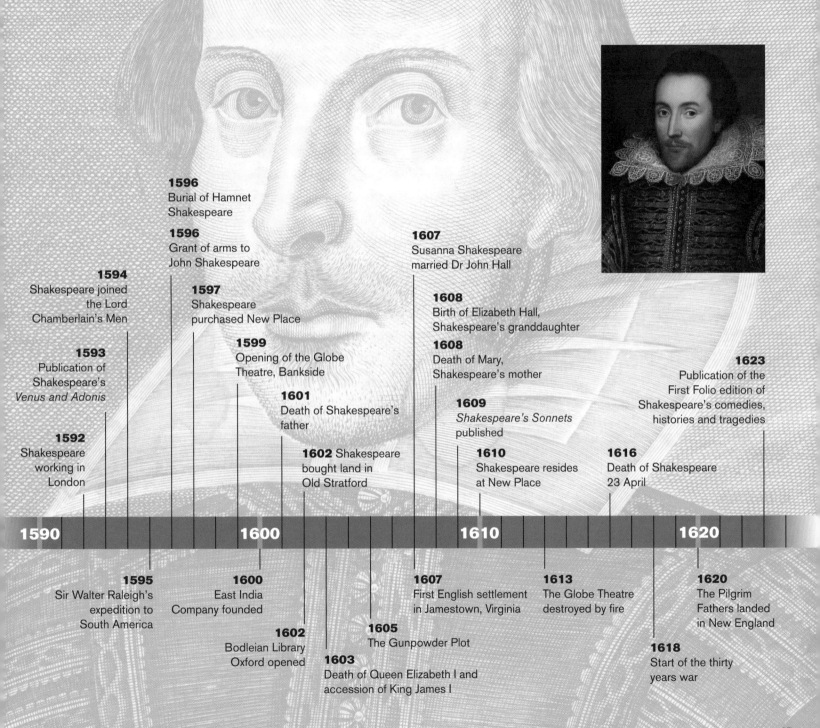

1596
Burial of Hamnet Shakespeare

1596
Grant of arms to John Shakespeare

1607
Susanna Shakespeare married Dr John Hall

1594
Shakespeare joined the Lord Chamberlain's Men

1597
Shakespeare purchased New Place

1608
Birth of Elizabeth Hall, Shakespeare's granddaughter

1593
Publication of Shakespeare's *Venus and Adonis*

1599
Opening of the Globe Theatre, Bankside

1608
Death of Mary, Shakespeare's mother

1623
Publication of the First Folio edition of Shakespeare's comedies, histories and tragedies

1601
Death of Shakespeare's father

1609
Shakespeare's Sonnets published

1592
Shakespeare working in London

1602 Shakespeare bought land in Old Stratford

1610
Shakespeare resides at New Place

1616
Death of Shakespeare 23 April

1590   **1600**   **1610**   **1620**

1595
Sir Walter Raleigh's expedition to South America

1600
East India Company founded

1607
First English settlement in Jamestown, Virginia

1613
The Globe Theatre destroyed by fire

1620
The Pilgrim Fathers landed in New England

1602
Bodleian Library Oxford opened

1605
The Gunpowder Plot

1618
Start of the thirty years war

1603
Death of Queen Elizabeth I and accession of King James I

Did Shakespeare write Shakespeare?

President of The Shakespeare Birthplace Trust, Professor Stanley Wells CBE, is often asked this question. Here is his response.

'A mass of evidence from Shakespeare's own time shows that a man called William Shakespeare wrote the plays and poems of William Shakespeare. Title pages of early editions of many of his plays and poems name him as their author. There are references to Shakespeare in works by other writers such as Francis Meres, who in 1598 named Shakespeare as the author of twelve plays.

Explicit evidence that the Shakespeare who wrote the plays was the man of Stratford-upon-Avon is provided by his monument in Holy Trinity Church, which compares the man of Stratford with great figures of antiquity, and by Ben Jonson's verses in the First Folio, which call him the "sweet swan of Avon". There is nothing to show that anyone doubted Shakespeare's authorship until the middle of the 19th century.'

Find out more: www.shakespeare.org.uk

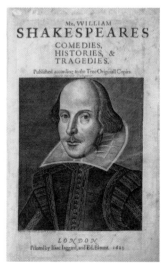

The First Folio.

Recommended reading

Words, words, words

(*Hamlet* Act 2, Scene 2)

The *Oxford Shakespeare* is the best all-round, single, complete edition where you will get a radical and authoritative version of the plays and poems. The *Penguin Shakespeare* provides the most accessible versions of the individual plays.

The Oxford Companion to Shakespeare,
    edited by Stanley Wells and Michael Dobson

Jonathan Bate, *The Genius of Shakespeare*

Andrew Dickson, *The Rough Guide to Shakespeare*

Paul Edmondson and Stanley Wells, *Shakespeare's Sonnets*

Germaine Greer, *Shakespeare's Wife*

James Shapiro, *Contested Will: Who Wrote Shakespeare?*

J. C. Trewin, *The Pocket Companion to Shakespeare's Plays*

René Weis, *Shakespeare Revealed*

Stanley Wells, *Is it True What They Say About Shakespeare?*

Michael Wood, *In Search of Shakespeare*

As truth's authentic author to be cited...

(*Troilus and Cressida* Act 3, Scene 2)

The chronology of Shakespeare's works

The Two Gentlemen of Verona	**1590–91**	Hamlet		**1600–1601**
The Taming of the Shrew	**1590–91**	Twelfth Night, or What You Will		**1600–1601**
Henry VI, Part II	**1591**	The Phoenix and the Turtle (poem)	by	**1601**
Henry VI, Part III	**1591**	Troilus and Cressida		**1602**
Henry VI, Part I (perhaps with Thomas Nashe)	**1592**	The Sonnets (poems)		**1582–1602**
Titus Andronicus (perhaps with George Peele)	**1592**	Measure for Measure		**1603**
Richard III	**1592–93**	A Lover's Complaint (poem)		**1603–04**
Venus and Adonis (poem)	**1592–93**	Sir Thomas More		**1603–04**
The Rape of Lucrece (poem)	**1593–94**	Othello		**1603–04**
The Comedy of Errors	**1594**	All's Well That Ends Well		**1604–05**
Love's Labour's Lost	**1594–95**	Timon of Athens (with Thomas Middleton)		**1605**
Edward III (authorship uncertain)	printed in **1596**	King Lear		**1605–06**
Richard II	**1595**	Macbeth (revised by Middleton)		**1606**
Romeo and Juliet	**1595**	Antony and Cleopatra		**1606**
A Midsummer Night's Dream	**1595**	Pericles (with George Wilkins)		**1607**
King John	**1596**	Coriolanus		**1608**
The Merchant of Venice	**1596–97**	The Winter's Tale		**1609**
Henry IV, Part I	**1596–97**	Cymbeline		**1610**
The Merry Wives of Windsor	**1597–98**	The Tempest		**1611**
Henry IV, Part II	**1597–98**	Henry VIII (by Shakespeare and John Fletcher; known in its own time as All is True)		**1613**
Much Ado About Nothing	**1598**	Cardenio (by Shakespeare and Fletcher; lost)		**1613**
Henry V	**1598–99**	The Two Noble Kinsmen (by Shakespeare and Fletcher)		**1613–14**
Julius Caesar	**1599**			
As You Like It	**1599–1600**